W9-DAD-698

Charles
DARWIN

Cath Senker

RAINTREE
STECK-VAUGHN
PUBLISHERS

A Harcourt Company

Austin   New York
www.raintreesteckvaughn.com

© Copyright 2002, text, Steck-Vaughn Company

Published by Raintree Steck-Vaughn Publishers, an imprint of Steck-Vaughn Company

Library of Congress Cataloging-in-Publication Data

Senker, Cath.
    Charles Darwin / Cath Senker.
       p. cm. -- (Scientists who made history)
    Includes bibliographical references and index.
    ISBN 0-7398-4843-7
    1. Darwin, Charles, 1809-1882--Juvenile literature.
    2. Naturalists--England--Biography--Juvenile literature.
    [1. Darwin, Charles, 1809-1882. 2. Naturalists.] I. Title
    II. Series.

    QH31.D2 S46 2001
    576.8'092--dc21
    [B]   2001019862

Printed in Italy. Bound in the United States.

1 2 3 4 5 6 7 8 9 0 LB 06 05 04 03 02

Picture Acknowledgments: AKG 24, 30, 33; Bridgeman 10, 14b, 21, 22, 35t, 37; Bruce Coleman 4, 5, 14t, 16t&b, 32, 35b, 41b; Cambridgeshire Collection, Cambridge Central Library 11b; Darwin Archive, by permission of the Syndics of Cambridge University Library 38; Mary Evans 6, 7, 9b, 13, 15, 17, 18, 26, 29, 31, 34, 36, 39t&b, 42; Fotomas Index 11t, 20t, 25; Hodder Wayland Picture Library 8t&b, 19t&b, 20b, 28, 40; Oxford Scientific Films 27; Popperfoto 40, 41t; Chris Schwarz 43; Topham 41; University College London 23 (Galton papers 9).

Contents

Mysterious Islands

"We landed upon black, dismal-looking heaps of broken lava, forming a shore fit for pandemonium [wild disorder]. Innumerable crabs and hideous iguanas started in every direction as we scrambled from rock to rock."

ROBERT FITZROY, CAPTAIN OF THE H.M.S. *BEAGLE*, IN HIS MEMOIRS OF THE JOURNEY.

IT WAS SEPTEMBER 15, 1835, when the H.M.S. *Beagle* reached Chatham, one of the Galápagos Islands in the Pacific Ocean, 650 miles (1,046 km) west of Ecuador. A young British naturalist by the name of Charles Darwin and the crew of the ship were nearing the end of a five-year voyage around the world.

At first sight, Chatham Island seemed like an ugly, uninviting place. The crew looked upon vast heaps of black volcanic rock on the shore. Dozens of volcanoes rose 100 feet (30 m) into the air. The ground was covered with black cinders. Darwin found them burning hot and painful to walk on. The air was warm and sticky, and there was an unpleasant smell.

But if it was hell for humans, the island appeared to be a

BELOW: *A view of one of the Galápagos Islands today, with a volcano in the background and a seal basking in the shallows. The black rocks are volcanic, made from the hardened lava from a volcano.*

paradise for huge reptiles. Turtles glided around the bay. Farther inland, there were giant tortoises 13 feet (4 m) in circumference, plodding around clumsily and munching on prickly pears. Vast numbers of marine iguanas—strange, seaweed-eating creatures—slept on the shoreline rocks.

The birds on the island were tame—they obviously had no predators. Darwin poked at a hawk with the barrel of his gun and it simply gazed at him. Hunting would not be very challenging here. The crew shot eighteen giant tortoises easily and hauled them aboard to eat as fresh meat.

After five weeks of traveling around the Galápagos islands, the *Beagle*'s crew members were glad to leave this strange, uncomfortable place. As he dined on tortoise meat over the next few weeks, Darwin had little idea that these hostile islands would provide later the key to his new and different theories of evolution.

BELOW: *An adult marine iguana with its young on its back. At the time Darwin visited the Galápagos islands, scientists believed that marine iguanas came from mainland South America. Later, Darwin realized that these animals were found only on the Galápagos and nowhere else.*

DARWIN'S WORLD

When Darwin was born, at the beginning of the 19th century, most people in Britain still lived in the countryside. They worked on farms or in small businesses. Most were also Christians, who went to church on Sundays and believed in God. The common view was that everyone had their place in life. The ruling class, led by the king, owned most of the land and held most of the power. Then there were many ranks, down through the middle classes, to the poorest, landless farmworkers. People believed that society was fixed by God and could not be changed. Scientists usually made sure their discoveries fit in with the Bible, too.

BELOW: *An illustration of the opening of the Stockton-to-Darlington railway, England, in 1825. The growth of the railways was an important part of Britain's Industrial Revolution. Goods could now be moved quickly and cheaply around the country by train.*

ABOVE: *Machinery being used in a stocking factory in Tewkesbury, England, in 1860. You can see lists of rules for the workers on the right-hand wall. By bringing together many workers in one place who used machinery, factories could produce larger amounts of goods than when people made them by hand.*

Yet Britain in the early 1800s was changing rapidly. The steam engine had been invented in the 18th century and factories, powered by steam, were being set up to make goods quickly and cheaply. This was the beginning of the Industrial Revolution.

Society was beginning to change, too. A growing middle class of people, who invested in the new industries, needed practical inventions. These would help them to develop new ways of making things. They wanted science based on experiments rather than religious beliefs. Working people were also starting to question the biblical view of the world.

IN THEIR OWN WORDS

"That which hath been is that which will be. And that which has been done is that which will be done. So there is nothing new under the sun."

FROM THE BOOK OF ECCLESIASTES IN THE OLD TESTAMENT OF THE BIBLE, WHICH SUMS UP THE CHURCH OF ENGLAND'S VIEW OF THE WORLD IN THE 19TH CENTURY.

Early Years

CHARLES ROBERT DARWIN was born on February 12, 1809, near Shrewsbury, England. His father, Robert, was a doctor, and his mother, Susannah, was the daughter of Josiah Wedgwood, who built up the famous Wedgwood pottery industry. Charles was the fifth of six children in this wealthy, middle-class family.

As a young boy, Charles loved to wander off on his own around the grounds of the family's huge home, called The Mount. His father loved plants, so there were exotic fruit trees and rare shrubs to discover, and his mother kept unusual pigeons. A mischievous child, one of Charles' earliest memories was of trying to break the window in a room he had been locked in as a punishment.

ABOVE: *A portrait of Charles' grandfather, Erasmus Darwin (1731–1802). Erasmus had his own early theories about evolution, which he published in a book called* Zoonomia. *In the book, Erasmus described his ideas about how the environment affects living things.*

LEFT: *A portrait of Charles' father, Robert Darwin. Robert thought that Charles spent too much time on his hobbies and did not study hard enough.*

LEFT: *A drawing of Charles with his sister Catherine, who was about five-years-old. Charles was interested in nature from an early age, which you can see by the plant he is holding.*

Charles loved to spend hours fishing in the river, using worms he'd collected himself for bait. Collecting things was Charles' greatest hobby. All sorts of things fascinated him, from shells, to birds' eggs and postal marks, or franks.

His mother died when Charles was eight, and from then on he was brought up by his father and three older sisters. The atmosphere at home was tense. All lived in fear of their father, with his strict rules of behavior.

In 1818, when Charles was nine-years-old he was sent to boarding school. He was extremely bored by the lessons and he didn't do well in school. He enjoyed his hobbies far more than his schoolwork. One year, Charles and his brother Erasmus took an interest in chemistry. They set up a laboratory in the garden shed and created lots of smelly gases. As a teenager, one of Charles' favorite pastimes was going hunting.

IN THEIR OWN WORDS

"[Charles would] invent deliberate falsehoods... for the pure pleasure of exciting attention and surprise."

JOSIAH WEDGWOOD, DESCRIBING DARWIN AS A BOY.

BLOOD, GUTS, AND BOTANY

In 1825, at the age of 16, Charles Darwin was sent off to Edinburgh University in Scotland to study medicine. His father had decided that Charles would follow in his own footsteps and become a doctor. Charles went to Edinburgh with his brother, Erasmus, who was also studying medicine. The two young men thought that the city of Edinburgh was beautiful, and they enjoyed the drinking and gambling that was part of student life.

Charles absolutely hated medicine, however. He found the lectures dull and he couldn't bear the horrors of surgery. In the early 19th century, surgeons in dirty clothing hacked off limbs with filthy saws, while the patients screamed in agony. During a particularly bad operation on a child, Charles walked out, vowing never again to enter an operating room.

BELOW: *An 18th-century illustration of a man having his leg amputated while student doctors watch from the right. It was not until the 1840s that patients were given anesthetic gases to breathe in order to dull the pain.*

LEFT: *Darwin's rooms were on the first floor of this building at Christ's College, Cambridge University.*

THE DIVINE DESIGNER

At the time Charles Darwin was studying at Cambridge, the most popular theory about how the natural world was formed was by the Reverend William Paley. He argued that things in nature were so perfectly designed for their role in life that they could not possibly have come into being by themselves. There had to have been a divine creator, which was God. This theory also conformed with the Creation story in the Bible, which said that God created the world and everything in it in seven days. As a student, Darwin accepted Paley's argument, but he soon saw the problems with it.

BELOW: *An engraving showing the view from Darwin's rooms at Christ's College, Cambridge, where he studied for three years. Darwin liked going to John Henslow's botany lectures and was constantly asking him questions about plants.*

Cambridge

In 1828, Charles moved to Cambridge University to study to become a clergyman in the Church of England. His father believed this would be a good job for an aimless son. It would provide a comfortable living, too. As a clergyman, Charles would have a fine country home with a few acres of land, and could spend much of his time enjoying his favorite hobbies of collecting plants and animals, and hunting.

At Cambridge, Darwin became friendly with the geologist Adam Sedgwick and botanist John Henslow, and his interest in rocks, animals, and plants grew. He joined the beetle craze, which consisted of wealthy young gentlemen traveling around the country looking for rare and unusual beetles to add to their collections. Yet Darwin studied hard enough to pass his exams at Cambridge, and in 1831 he was awarded a Bachelor of Arts degree.

The Voyage of the *Beagle*

BELOW, MAIN MAP: *The Beagle's route. From England, the ship crossed the Atlantic and made several trips up and down the coasts of South America, before sailing west across the Pacific to New Zealand and Australia.*
INSET MAP: *Darwin's Britain, showing the places he lived.*

THE TIME WAS RIPE for Darwin to become a clergyman and settle down. But he didn't feel ready yet. He had just read Alexander Humboldt's *Personal Narrative*, in which the writer described a fascinating voyage he made around South America from 1799 to 1804. Darwin decided that the discovery of lush, tropical forests and rugged volcanoes was just the thing for him.

In August 1831, Darwin was offered a position on the H.M.S. *Beagle*. The captain, Robert FitzRoy, was about to set sail for South America on a two-year mission to make maps for the Royal Navy. Darwin would be the ship's naturalist and companion to the captain. Darwin's father was horrified at this reckless plan and refused to pay for the trip. But his closest friend and brother-in-law Jos Wedgwood persuaded him to let his son go. Darwin was overjoyed.

0   150 miles
0   200 kilometers

SCOTLAND
Edinburgh ■

ENGLAND

Shrewsbury ●
Cambridge ●
London ■
KENT

N

PACIFIC OCEAN

ATLANTIC OCEAN

ENGLAND

Galápagos Islands

BRAZIL

ECUADOR

CHILE

ARGENTINA

INDIAN OCEAN

Cape of Good Hope

AUSTRALIA

NEW ZEALAND

Straits of Magellan

Tierra del Fuego

Cape Horn

H.M.S. BEAGLE
MIDDLE SECTION FORE AND AFT
1832

UPPER DECK
1832

LEFT: *This drawing shows the layout of the* Beagle. *The ship was tiny—only 89 feet (27 m) long and 24 feet (7.3 m) wide. Darwin shared a cabin with one of the officers. He slept in a hammock above the chart table.*

Seasickness and Specimens

In December, the H.M.S. *Beagle* set sail, and Darwin's misery began straight away. He was horribly seasick. For ten days he could keep no food down except dry biscuits and raisins. He was to suffer from seasickness throughout the voyage.

Darwin's spirits perked up when the *Beagle* arrived in South America. They landed at Salvador in Bahia, Brazil, and Darwin set foot in an amazing world. He was completely amazed by the thick vegetation, fantastic flowers, and countless varieties of insects.

While on his travels, Darwin shipped back vast quantities of specimens, which provided great excitement for scientists back in Britain. Among the specimens were many fossils, including part of the fossil of an extinct giant sloth called Megatherium, and a giant llama-like creature. These finds started Darwin wondering why those animals had died out, and how they might be related to similar animals that still existed.

FOSSILS

In Darwin's time, the accepted view of fossils came from the Creation story in the Bible. It was believed that all fossils were formed at the same time, after one great disaster such as Noah's flood, which wiped out most living things. But the evidence from the rocks showed that fossils from nearer the surface were more similar to animals and plants living in the present day than those from deeper layers. It seemed that the earlier animals and plants had gradually died out, to be replaced by others. But until Darwin's groundbreaking theory, no one knew exactly how this happened.

Fish fossil from layer nearer the surface.

Ammonite fossil from a deeper layer.

INCREDIBLE CHANGING WORLD

During the *Beagle* voyage, Darwin saw dramatic things that started him imagining about how things might change in the natural world. He puzzled over why animals and plants varied in different areas. For example, in Patagonia, there were two varieties of rhea (ostrich-like birds), living in different parts of the country. Why were there two varieties and why had they separated? The mysteries of the fossils added to the puzzle. Long-dead plants and animals were similar but not the same as those living in the present.

While on board, Darwin read Charles Lyell's *Principles of Geology*, which was published in 1830. Lyell wrote that all the processes of nature, such as coastal erosion, go on at the same rate, so they must have been going on for millions of years. Over an extremely long time, they shaped the earth we see today.

ABOVE: *This bird is a greater rhea. Darwin saw two types of rhea in the Galápagos: greater and smaller. At first, Darwin wondered if one type of rhea had been born from the other, as a kind of "freak," and had gone on to create a new species. He later realized that they had both evolved into different species.*

BELOW: *An engraving of the* Beagle *in the Straits of Magellan, which cut through the southern tip of South America. Local people from Tierra del Fuego are shown in three dug-out canoes around the ship.*

Later, in 1835, Darwin witnessed a terrible earthquake in Chile. Earthquakes are caused when huge pressures under the earth build up over time, and then are suddenly released. Pondering over the earthquake, Darwin started thinking that if the landscape had been changing throughout history, then living things also must have changed.

People seemed to look different as well. In December 1832, the *Beagle* landed at Tierra del Fuego, at the southernmost tip of South America. Captain FitzRoy wanted to return three Fuegians (people from Tierra del Fuego), who had been living in England. Darwin was shocked to see the local Fuegians. They wore few clothes, painted their faces, and slept on the wet ground. How were they related to an educated Englishman like himself?

IN THEIR OWN WORDS

"When we were on the shore, the party looked rather alarmed, but continued talking and making gestures with great rapidity. It was without exception the most curious and interesting spectacle I had ever beheld. I could not have believed how wide was the difference between savage and civilized man. It is greater than that between a wild and domesticated animal, in as much as in man there is a greater power of improvement."

DARWIN IN 1832, FROM THE DIARY
HE WROTE ON HIS VOYAGE.

RIGHT: *An engraving made in about 1860 showing indigenous people from Tierra del Fuego.*

GALÁPAGOS ISLANDS

In September 1835, the *Beagle* left the west coast of South America and set off across the Pacific Ocean. About 625 miles (1,000 km) from the mainland city of Lima, Peru, the ship reached a group of around thirteen small, rocky volcanic islands—the Galápagos Islands. This was a short, five-week stop near the end of a long and exhausting voyage. But it was to have great significance for Darwin's theory of evolution.

The huge reptiles and strange birds of the Galápagos were like no others that Darwin had ever come across. Yet they seemed to have some things in common with species on the South American mainland. What was the relationship between them?

More curious was the fact that each island had its very own kinds of plants and animals, slightly different from the ones found on the other islands. Each had its own varieties of strange and beautiful orchids, and different kinds of finches. There were giant tortoises, large enough for the

ABOVE: *A Galápagos giant tortoise. Darwin later figured out that the prisoners on the Galápagos had been right— each island had its own type of tortoise. Each type was adapted to living on its own particular island.*

BELOW: *Bartholomew Island in the Galápagos. Today, the Galápagos Islands are protected as a nature reserve. Yet their unique plants and animals are under threat from the effects of tourism and pollution, such as a spill from an oil tanker in January 2001.*

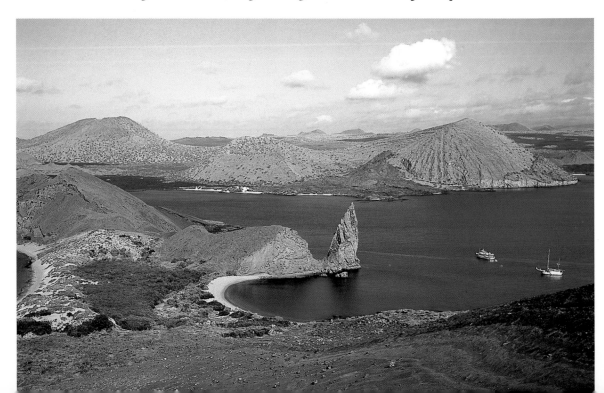

THE GALÁPAGOS FINCHES

The Galápagos finches provided a key to Darwin's theory of evolution. Found nowhere else in the world, each species of finch had a slightly different beak, which was suited to a particular kind of food.

The Galápagos Islands formed relatively recently in the history of Earth, just a few million years ago. A few finches probably landed there from the mainland of South America, perhaps blown to the islands in a storm. Food was plentiful. The original species of finch gradually evolved into many different species, each suited to eating a different kind of food. This meant that the birds did not compete with each other. The finches showed how, over time, species change to suit their environment.

Large ground finch has a huge beak for cracking tough seeds.

Medium ground finch has a smaller beak, for cracking smaller seeds.

Small ground finch has a small, strong beak for cracking small, hard seeds.

Warbler finch has a long, slim beak for probing into cracks in trees and catching insects.

ship's crew to ride like horses. A group of exiled prisoners from Ecuador, who were living on one of the islands, claimed they could tell which island a tortoise came from by the shape of its shell.

Back on board the *Beagle*, Darwin didn't bother labeling which islands all his different finch specimens came from. It was only when he got back to England that he realized the differences among the Galápagos animals were incredibly important.

ABOVE: *Illustrations of some of the different kinds of finches discovered by Darwin. This example of evolution has become so famous that the birds are often known as "Darwin's finches."*

COLONIZERS OR CIVILIZERS?

IN THEIR OWN WORDS

"[They were] clean, tidy, and healthy in appearance, like that of dairy maids in England...I never saw a nicer or more merry group, and to think that this was in the center of the land of cannibalism, murder, and all atrocious crimes!"

DARWIN, WRITING IN HIS DIARY ABOUT THE MAORI SERVANT GIRLS IN NEW ZEALAND.

THE NEXT LEG of the *Beagle's* journey took the crew to Tahiti, New Zealand, and Australia. To Darwin, Tahiti was a tropical paradise of bananas, coconuts, and breadfruit trees. Even delicious guavas grew everywhere, like weeds. Tahiti was an island where missionaries were established. European Christians went there to convert the local people to Christianity and guide them toward adopting a European lifestyle.

Darwin was impressed. He saw the "laughing merry faces" of the Tahitians, their neat clothes, and the friendly welcome they gave visitors. To his understanding, typical of a wealthy Victorian, this meant the Tahitians, using Europeans as their examples, were becoming more civilized. More questions came to mind. Did people develop over time, and if so, were earlier humans very different? This idea conflicted with the biblical view that people were a fixed type, created by God.

RIGHT: *An illustration from about 1850 of Hororwowa (left), a Maori chief in New Zealand who was converted to Christianity. Darwin firmly believed that it was right to make other peoples become Christians and adopt a European lifestyle. He felt it made them better, more civilized people.*

ABOVE: *This painting shows the arrival of the first governor of New South Wales in Sydney, Australia, on January 26, 1788. The governor is about to propose a toast to King George III of England, as the Union Jack flag is raised to show that the land is claimed by Great Britain.*

New Zealand and Australia

The next stop was New Zealand, where the local Maoris had suffered unspeakable horrors. Almost entirely wiped out by the Europeans taking over the country at the time, the few who remained were being forced to become Christians. In Australia, too, where the *Beagle* landed in January 1836, the indigenous Aborigines were being killed, or were dying from European diseases and lack of food. Darwin wondered whether the human world was just like the animal world, where the strong always seemed to destroy the weak. If God had created all the people in the world at the same time, as told in the Bible's Creation story, why did he make them all so different?

ABOVE: *A photograph of an Australian aborigine in front of his temporary shelter in the late 19th century.*

Home at Last

AFTER LEAVING AUSTRALIA in March 1836, Darwin was eager to get home. Seven months later, on the stormy night of October 2, 1836, the *Beagle* arrived in Falmouth, England. After his spectacular travels, Darwin faced the huge task of sorting out his finds, which included 1,529 species bottled in spirits and 3,907 labeled specimens. Just as importantly, he needed to think about all the questions that were whirling around inside his head. The real work was about to begin.

Using his 770-page diary and other journals, Darwin started work on a book about the events of the *Beagle* voyage, which he called the *Journal of Researches*. He also began writing other books on zoology and coral reefs.

Meanwhile he decided it was time to find a wife. Emma Wedgwood, his first cousin, had caught his eye. Both families approved of the match, and the couple married in 1838. Since Darwin's personal and working life were never far apart, he started writing in his notebooks about mating in animals. In 1839, Darwin published his *Journal of Researches*, which he'd been working on for the past three years.

ABOVE: *A case of beetles from Darwin's collection. Darwin had always been a careful collector. Keeping samples of plants and animals and writing notes about them were vital to his success as a scientist.*

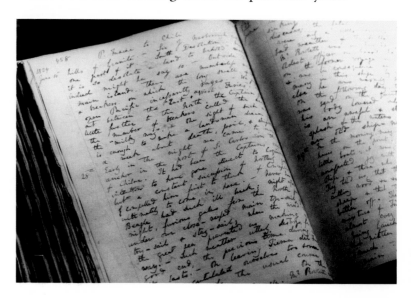

RIGHT: *Pages of Darwin's diary that he wrote while on the* Beagle's *voyage. Throughout his life, Darwin kept a personal diary in addition to writing notes on his research.*

ABOVE: *A portrait of Emma Darwin, shortly after her marriage to Charles.*

It was hugely successful.

Charles and Emma bought a house in Upper Gower Street, London. Their first child, William, was born in December 1839. As soon as Willy arrived, Darwin started taking notes on the baby's first signs of anger, fear, and pleasure. He was thinking about the origins of humans, and he wanted to compare his baby's expressions with the behavior of Jenny Orang, an orangutan in London Zoo.

After a few years, Darwin decided that London, with all its traffic and chaos, was no place to bring up a family. On September 17, 1842, he collected their valuables and slammed the door on 12 Upper Gower Street for the last time. The Darwins were moving to the country.

IN THEIR OWN WORDS

Marry

1. Children

2. Constant companion... object to be beloved and played with—better than a dog anyhow

3. Home, and someone to take care of house

4. ...it is intolerable to think of spending one's whole life...working, working, and nothing after all. Only picture to yourself a nice, soft wife on a sofa with a good fire, and books and music...

Not Marry

1. Freedom to go where one liked

2. Not forced to visit relatives...[or] to have the expense and anxiety of children

3. Loss of time...fatness and idleness

4. If many children, forced to gain one's bread [earn money]—(but then it is very bad for one's health to work too much)

A SHORTENED LIST OF THE PROS AND CONS THAT DARWIN WROTE WHEN CONSIDERING GETTING MARRIED.

LIFE IN THE COUNTRY

The Darwins' new home was Down House in Kent, the kind of country house Darwin had dreamed of when he was thinking of becoming a clergyman. Deep in the countryside, 7.5 miles (12 km) from the nearest railway station, it was ideal for a gentleman naturalist. In a letter to an old servant, Covington, he noted, "This will be my direction [address] for the rest of my life."

Over the following years, the Darwin family grew rapidly. Ten children were born to Charles and Emma, but three died in childhood. In mid-19th-century England, even the wealthy were not spared the tragedy of frequent childhood deaths.

BELOW: *Down House, the Darwins' home in Kent, as it is today. Darwin was a very private man. When the family moved into their new home, he had a wall built high enough around the property so that no one could look in.*

Emma was a devoted wife to Darwin, who demanded her constant attention. He couldn't bear for her to be away from him. Even when Emma's mother died in 1846, and she had to go away for a short while over the summer, Darwin fretted endlessly and complained of loneliness.

Darwin was a man who liked a peaceful life with a fixed routine. He didn't like visiting people and there were few guests at Down House. Darwin described his days there as being as alike "as two peas." He would get up at 7 A.M. and work until 10 A.M., when he and Emma would have breakfast and relax. Then he worked until lunch at 2 P.M. After lunch, he might go into town, returning for dinner and a quiet evening reading and listening to music. Most of Darwin's days were spent in this way.

IN THEIR OWN WORDS

"I am an ungracious old dog to howl, for I have been... thinking what a fortunate man I am, so well-off in worldly circumstances, with such dear little children and... more than all with such a wife."

DARWIN COUNTING HIS BLESSINGS DURING EMMA'S ABSENCE, IN THE SUMMER OF 1846.

A SICK MAN

"When relations unite...there is a decrease in general vigor."

DARWIN, IN *THE ORIGIN OF SPECIES*, ABOUT THE DANGERS OF INBREEDING WITHIN FAMILIES SUCH AS HIS OWN.

Darwin had been a healthy man during the *Beagle* voyage, tramping across the grassy South American plains and climbing mountains with ease. Once he returned to England, however, he became ill.

The illnesses Darwin suffered from were many and varied. They ranged from skin problems to headaches, stomach pains, and broken sleep. Often, he could only work a few hours a day. We know this from Darwin's careful records of the number of working days he lost due to illness. He couldn't take part fully in scientific debates because he never appeared in public. Yet he exchanged letters with many well-known scientists.

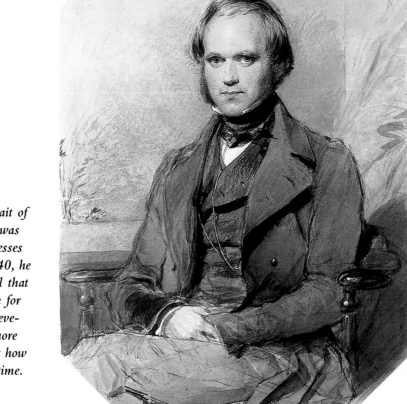

RIGHT: *A watercolor portrait of Darwin in 1840, when he was 31 years old. Darwin's illnesses made him miserable. In 1840, he complained to Charles Lyell that he hadn't been able to work for nine whole weeks. His achievements in science are even more amazing when you consider how ill he was for much of the time.*

There are several theories about Darwin's illnesses. Did he catch a tropical disease while traveling around the world? Did he have lots of allergies, or perhaps chronic fatigue syndrome—an illness that makes people very tired and depressed? Or was his ill-health brought on by stress?

Darwin was terrified that he had passed on his ill-health to his children, who were often ill, too. Various cures were attempted with mixed results.

In the late 1840s, when Darwin was about 40 years old, he was frail and barely able to walk. He tried a cure called hydropathy, which involved a special diet, taking homeopathic remedies which included small doses of medicine that produced symptoms resembling the disease being treated, and being scrubbed with cold water every day. The cure seemed to work at first, but the effects did not last, and Darwin was bothered by ill-health for the rest of his life.

BELOW: *A photograph of Darwin's microscope, which was one of his most important pieces of equipment. Another was his gun, which he used to shoot many of his animal specimens.*

A Theory Evolves

"I think I have found out (here's presumption!) the simple way by which species become exquisitely adapted to various ends."

DARWIN, WRITING TO HIS FRIEND, THE BOTANIST JOSEPH DALTON HOOKER, IN LATE 1843.

AT THIS TIME in Britain, most people believed in the biblical story of Creation. One churchman, Archbishop Usher, actually made calculations using the Bible that showed when the world was created, and came up with the date 4004 B.C. It was thought that human beings were special, made by God to be better than animals. But some people already had their doubts about the biblical version of events.

Geologists such as Charles Lyell had already shown that Earth was older than the Bible said. Fossils showed that some animals and plants had lived in the past but had died out. The fact that there were living animals and plants that were similar to species that had died out led some scientists to suggest that living things evolved, or changed over time.

BELOW: *Darwin's study in Down House, cluttered with books and papers. Darwin kept notebooks on different subjects, including his diary and secret notebooks where he wrote down his ideas about evolution long before making them public.*

DARWIN'S THEORY OF NATURAL SELECTION

Darwin's theory of evolution was that plants and animals change over time through a process of natural selection. It works like this:

1. Parents have young that are similar, but slightly different to themselves.

2. More young are born than can survive. The young with features that are better suited to their environment survive and breed.

3. The plants and animals that survive, breed, and pass on the useful features to their own young.

4. Over time, these tiny variations in features mean that species change.

5. Species that are best adapted to their environment do well. The ones that are poorly adapted die out.

Several scientists had come up with theories of evolution. Around 1800, French naturalist Jean-Baptiste Lamarck (1744–1829) developed the idea that animals could change depending on the environment they lived in. For example, giraffes needed to feed from high trees, so they grew longer necks. Then their babies were born with longer necks.

Since 1837, Darwin had secretly been building his own theory of evolution. He agreed with Lamarck that plants and animals had evolved. But he did not believe that they changed within their own lifetime and passed on the changes to their offspring. Darwin was the first to compile a believable theory about evolution.

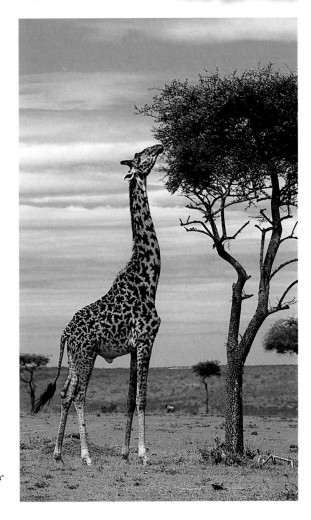

RIGHT: *A giraffe reaching for leaves in Kenya. We now know that the giraffe's long neck is set in its genes. They cannot change during the lifetime of one animal.*

DANGEROUS IDEAS

The more Darwin researched the evolution of the natural world, the more evidence he found that conflicted with the Creation story in the Bible. And if the Creation story was wrong, did that mean that other parts of the Bible—the basis of Christian beliefs—might be wrong too? Even though Darwin had developed his theory by 1842, he did not dare publish his ideas at first. He was terrified of the possible terrible effect it would have on English society. His social class, including all his good friends, was linked to the Church. Everyone would be horrified by a theory of Creation without God.

In the late 1830s and 1840s, a radical organization called the Chartists was making protests in Britain. The Chartists hated the common view that everyone had their place in life, decided by God. They wanted broad political changes, such as giving the vote to all men over the age of 21, not just to those who owned property. The fear of Chartist demonstrators rioting through the streets had been one of the reasons the Darwin family left London. Darwin worried that his theory of evolution would encourage radicals like

BELOW: *Dancing at a high society party in London, in the 19th century. Many wealthy people liked the idea that everyone had a fixed place in life, decided by God. Yet Darwin's theory showed that human beings had developed just like plants and other animals. No special power made them different from the rest of the natural world.*

LEFT: *A portrait of Joseph Dalton Hooker (1817–1911). At first, Hooker did not accept Darwin's ideas on evolution, but he was prepared to discuss them and to test them through his own research. Over time however, he became convinced that species could evolve into others, as Darwin suggested. Later, after Darwin published his theory of evolution, Hooker was one of his strongest supporters.*

the Chartists by helping them to argue that if the world was always changing, society could change, too.

Yet Darwin could not keep quiet forever. In 1844, he wrote an essay containing his main ideas about evolution and sent it to his good friend, the botanist Joseph Dalton Hooker, to read. Since Darwin was quite ill at the time, he instructed his wife to publish the essay if he died. He realized that his theory would have to come out one day, even if it meant turning his comfortable world upside down.

IN THEIR OWN WORDS

"I am almost convinced (quite contrary to the opinion I started with) that species are not (it is like confessing a murder) immutable [unchanging]."

DARWIN IN 1844, WRITING TO JOSEPH HOOKER ABOUT HIS THEORY OF EVOLUTION AND COMPARING TALKING ABOUT IT TO CONFESSING A MURDER.

TESTING TIMES

ABOVE: *Revolutionaries tear down the palace of King Louis Philippe of France, in the February 1848 uprising in Paris. The king lost his throne, and the new French government allowed the people to vote for the first time. Revolutions quickly spread to the Austrian and Prussian regions of Europe. It is not surprising that the wealthy classes in nearby England were worried by these events.*

Darwin realized that he needed solid evidence to persuade the world that evolution was a serious theory, and not a mad scheme to uproot the Church. So he worked incredibly hard in the late 1840s and '50s to find evidence for his ideas.

In 1846, Darwin began a long, difficult, and dull study of barnacles, which lasted for eight years. He used his findings to show how natural selection worked in practice. Darwin spent so much time with these little creatures that his children began to think it was normal for everyone's father to study barnacles.

The year of 1848 was one of revolutions in Europe and huge Chartist demonstrations in England. The European revolutions were democratic movements, mostly led by the middle classes, which wanted to have a say in government. The working classes joined them, having become tired of a life of poverty, ruled by kings and queens living in extreme wealth. Shortly after an uprising in Paris in February, the Chartists planned a protest of 150,000 people in London. Panic spread among the wealthy classes.

By the end of the year, all the uprisings had been suppressed. Yet Darwin's worries about the radical theory he was nursing kept his stress levels high. To add to the pressure Darwin faced, in 1850, his much-loved oldest daughter Annie became ill, and she died in 1851. Darwin was devastated. Her death put an end to his already shaken faith in Christianity and he could no longer believe in a just world.

BELOW: *In April 1848 the Chartist demonstration was held on Kennington Common, London. The Chartists demonstrated to try to get the government to listen to their demands.*

IN THEIR OWN WORDS

"She hardly ever required to be found fault with, and was never punished in any way whatever… every expression in her countenance [face] beamed with affection and kindness, and all her habits were influenced by her loving disposition [nature]… Oh that she could now know how deeply, how tenderly we do still and shall ever love her dear joyous face. Blessings on her."

DARWIN, WRITING ABOUT HIS DAUGHTER ANNIE IN 1851, A WEEK AFTER SHE DIED.

COLLECTING AND SELECTING

In 1854, after putting away the barnacles, Darwin set up more experiments to try out his theory of natural selection. Friends, other scientists, and his own children helped out. Darwin decided to investigate domestic animals. Down House stank of duck meat as Darwin boiled up the animals' bodies to compare the skeletons of wild ducks with those of domestic ones.

No other gentleman scientist had done this kind of research since it was seen as rather undignified to get one's hands dirty messing around with farm animals. But Darwin realized that when people bred animals, their work might be similar to the process of evolution in nature.

He spent time in pubs and taverns talking to working-class pigeon breeders, who could spot the tiniest variation in the size of a pigeon's tail. For example, by breeding pigeons with the broadest tail feathers, over time the breeders had produced the fantail pigeon. They had created so many differences within domestic pigeons that if the pigeons were found in the wild, they would be classed as completely different species.

IN THEIR OWN WORDS

"...to the very root and foundation of his nature, man is one with the rest of the organic [natural] world."

THOMAS HUXLEY, IN A LECTURE IN MARCH 1858, ARGUING THAT HUMANS HAD EVOLVED FROM APES.

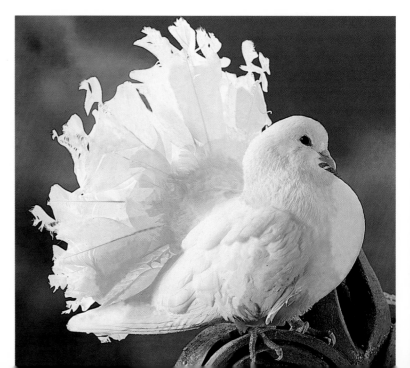

RIGHT: *A hen-white exhibition fantail pigeon. Working-class men in Darwin's time took pride in raising prize pigeons as a hobby. Darwin paid many of them to help him out with his research, and they welcomed his interest in their hobby. In the clubs of Borough, in south London, he became known as the "Squire."*

LEFT: *A photograph of Darwin in 1863, taken from the second edition of* The Origin of Species. *Darwin encouraged young scientists such as Hooker and Huxley, who began to get important jobs in science in the 1850s. They helped to spread new scientific ideas that did not fit in with the biblical view of the world.*

Here was more evidence for Darwin's theory of natural selection. Breeders used artificial selection. They mated animals according to particular features they wanted passed on to their young. It seemed they were simply speeding up what happened in nature anyway.

By the mid-1850s, Darwin had a few close friends who were starting to accept his views on evolution. Besides Joseph Hooker, young scientists Thomas Huxley and Alfred Russel Wallace shared some of his ideas. By 1856, Darwin felt brave enough to start writing a book for publication.

IN THEIR OWN WORDS

"I cannot swallow Man [being that] distinct from a chimpanzee... I wonder what a chimpanzee would say to this?"

DARWIN IN 1857, RESPONDING TO CHRISTIAN SCIENTIST RICHARD OWEN'S CLAIM THAT HUMANS WERE IN A SEPARATE CLASS FROM ANIMALS.

The Secret's Out!

IN 1858, DARWIN was still working on his huge book on evolution when, all of a sudden, the bottom dropped out of his world. On June 18, he received a letter from fellow scientist Alfred Russel Wallace. Inside, Wallace described how evolution occurred, in words close to Darwin's own.

Darwin was friends with Wallace and had shared ideas with him. But if Wallace's theory came out first, Darwin's work would not seem original and twenty years of work would be wasted. Success would go to the man who published first: Wallace. Yet Wallace had sent him the work in trust and Darwin could not betray him.

There was no choice. They would have to publish together—and fast. On June 30, Darwin and Wallace's joint paper on the theory of evolution was presented at a meeting of the Linnean Society, a scientific society in London. Surprisingly, the paper was greeted with silence and lack of interest. The President of the Linnean Society walked out of the meeting, disappointed. He later made a statement that the year had not been marked by any "striking discoveries." Darwin was

RIGHT: *A photograph of the British naturalist Alfred Russel Wallace (1823–1913). While in the Spice Islands of Indonesia, Wallace developed his theory of evolution, which was similar to that of Darwin. The two naturalists continued to debate the theory of evolution and remained friends for the rest of their lives.*

LEFT: *The first edition of* The Origin of Species, *published in 1859, which is now kept in the Natural History Museum, London. By 1871, six editions had been published. Darwin's book was translated into several languages, including Dutch, French, Italian, and German.*

not at the meeting. He and Emma were at the funeral of their baby son, Charles, who had just died of scarlet fever.

The Origin of Species

Despite the lack of interest from the Linnean Society, Darwin continued work on his book and in 1859, *On The Origin of Species by Means of Natural Selection* was finally published. It described how the process of natural selection made species evolve. All species were created and changed by nature. God was not involved. Darwin awaited the reaction to his theory with bated breath, fearing he would be cast out of polite society forever.

RIGHT: *The fossil of an archaeopteryx, discovered in Germany in 1861. This creature had a reptile's bones and tail—and feathers—showing that birds had reptile ancestors, and helping to prove that living things evolved from one form into another.*

"MOST DANGEROUS MAN IN ENGLAND"

The publisher of *The Origin of Species*, John Murray, was so worried about the fuss that the book would cause that he only printed 1,250 copies. They sold out almost right away as a fierce debate began throughout society.

Christians were outraged. Charles Darwin was denying that God had created the natural world and claimed that the biblical Creation story was untrue! Darwin knew that enemies like Richard Owen would hate his views, but others such as Adam Sedgwick, his Cambridge professor friend, also turned against him. One newspaper review labeled Darwin as "the most dangerous man in England."

Yet some people were full of praise. Darwin's scientist friends Huxley, Hooker, and Lyell formed a close circle of supporters. The pro-Darwin and the anti-Darwin camps now battled over evolution theory.

RIGHT: *A cartoon published in 1874 showing Darwin holding a mirror in front of an ape, to show how alike they are. After the publication of* **The Origin of Species,** *many popular newspapers wrote that Darwin was suggesting that people had evolved from living apes, such as gorillas. They were wrong.*

LEFT: *A drawing of the British naturalist Thomas Henry Huxley (1825–95) holding a skull in his hand. Huxley fought hard to establish himself as a scientist and became an enthusiastic supporter of Darwin's theory of evolution. He firmly believed that religion should be kept out of science. Huxley believed that human beings evolved directly from apes, which we now know is not true.*

In 1860, there was a famous showdown during a scientific debate in Oxford. The big debate had Bishop Samuel Wilberforce, nicknamed "Soapy Sam," defending God's role in the Creation of life. He was determined to "smash Darwin." On the other side were Darwin's supporters, Hooker and Huxley, fired up with determination to win the argument for natural selection. In a meeting crammed with about a thousand people, Darwin's supporters won the debate hands down.

The truth was that by 1860, the argument about evolution had been going on for a long time. Many people no longer believed the exact words of the Bible that said that God had created the world. They were looking for real, scientific answers to the mysteries of life, and were ready to accept Darwin's ideas.

A HERO AT LAST

Within a short time, most scientists came to accept Darwin's evolution theory. Thomas Huxley worked hard to spread Darwin's ideas in society. A natural teacher, he lectured to hundreds of working people on the origins of humans. The working classes welcomed proof that their status in life was not fixed by God.

Darwin was also popular abroad. He received various awards from countries including France, Germany, and Russia. The Germans were especially excited by Darwin, and *The Origin of Species* sold well there.

Apart from his constant illness, Darwin's life became more settled. The daily routine at Down House went on as ever and the children were growing up. All Darwin's sons went on to have excellent careers and his daughter Henrietta helped him with some of his work.

The aging scientist continued to write books throughout the 1860s and '70s. In 1871, eleven years after the publication of *The Origin of Species*, another book on evolution, *The Descent of Man,* was published. Here, Darwin made it clear that humans had evolved like other animals.

RIGHT: *The Darwin family at home at Down House, Kent, in 1863. From left to right: Leonard, Henrietta, Horace, Emma, Elizabeth, Francis, and a visitor. Henrietta Darwin helped her father write* The Descent of Man *and was later the editor of* Emma Darwin: A Century of Family Letters, *which was first published in 1904.*

ABOVE: *A photo of Emma Darwin in later years. She continued to care for Darwin right to the end, and accepted his death calmly.*

The idea no longer came as a shock to his readers. He also wrote a fascinating book describing facial and bodily expressions in animals and people. Several books on plants and one on worms followed as a result of Darwin's experiments in his garden.

In 1881, Darwin fell ill and in April 1882, at the age of 73, he died a painful death in Emma's loving arms. By this time, he had become an honored figure in British society, and was buried in Westminster Abbey. But Darwin hadn't cared for honors. It was more important to him that his theories survived him.

SEXUAL SELECTION

According to Darwin's theory of natural selection, the features of a living thing, such as its size, shape, and color, evolve to increase its chances of survival. But certain features, such as the peacock's colorful tail feathers, seem to reduce its chances by attracting predators. Darwin said that such features were an important part of sexual selection. The peacock's tail feathers help to attract female peahens so they can breed. Breeding successfully is part of survival.

ABOVE: *A photo of Darwin in later years. He continued working right up until his death in 1882.*

The Legacy of Darwin

ABOVE: *A laboratory worker in Israel, in June 2000, carrying out genetic research. By 2000, a rough map of all the genes that make up a human being had been completed.*

DARWIN'S THEORY OF EVOLUTION was a wonderful gift to science. It helped scientists to group both animals and plants according to their common ancestor. They could now examine living things by looking at what each feature was for, and how it helped the plant or animal to survive and breed.

Fossils were no longer a mystery. They were the remains of dead plants and animals. Most had died out, while others had evolved into new species. Scientists could trace the pattern of evolution by looking at how fossils changed over time.

One thing that puzzled Darwin was how features are passed on from parent to offspring. While Darwin was working on *The Origin of Species*, a monk named Gregor Mendel was experimenting with peas in what is now Brno, in the Czech Republic. He worked out how features are passed on from one generation to the next, through what we now call genes. It wasn't until around 1900 that the importance of his work was recognized.

MENDEL'S DISCOVERIES

Mendel studied how features in peas were passed on from generation to generation. One of the features he tested was color.

1. Mendel crossed plants that produced yellow peas with plants that produced green peas.

2. All the plants in the next generation produced yellow peas. The green peas seemed to have disappeared.

3. The yellow peas were planted and produced the next generation.

4. Of the "grandchildren" of the original pea plants, three-quarters produced yellow peas, and one-quarter produced green peas.

Mendel had discovered that the color of peas is decided by two pieces of information, passed on from the two parents. There is a "factor" for green and a "factor" for yellow. The yellow factor is dominant, so if the yellow factor is there at all, the plant will make yellow peas. If only the green factor is there, it will make green peas.

IN THEIR OWN WORDS

"No working biologist can read and understand Darwin's work without realizing the overwhelming importance it has had for the development of biological thought."

JONATHAN HOWARD, FELLOW OF THE
ROYAL SOCIETY, 1982.

LEFT: *In 1996, scientists produced a clone (exact copy) of a sheep, which had the same genes as its mother. They named the sheep Dolly. She became the world's first clone of a mammal.*

The study of how features are passed on became the science of genetics, which remains one of the hottest topics in science today. Since the 1980s, it has been discovered that the genetic material of humans differs by only 1 or 2 percent from the genetic material of gorillas and chimpanzees. We are 98–99 percent ape and only 1–2 percent purely human. This evidence would have delighted Darwin, who realized that apes were our close relatives.

BELOW: *A female chimpanzee teaching her young what to eat. Darwin noticed that in many ways, young chimpanzees behave like human children.*

IN THEIR OWN WORDS

"The growth of large business is merely the survival of the fittest. It is merely the working out of a law of nature."

U.S. BUSINESSMAN, JOHN D. ROCKEFELLER (1839–1937), EXPLAINING HIS SUCCESS USING THE THEORY OF SOCIAL DARWINISM.

DARWINISM IN QUESTION

Many people, however, have never accepted Darwin's theory of evolution. Some Christians believe that every word of the Bible is true. According to their beliefs, the world is only a few thousand years old, as it says in the Bible. The fossils were placed on Earth by God. We are not related to apes because humans are special and did not come from animal origins. To these believers, evolution theory is simply a theory that has not been proven.

Social Darwinism

Darwin did not apply his theory of evolution to human society. But later thinkers took up his ideas and used them to try to explain why people in society are not equal. In the mid-1860s, Herbert Spencer, a fellow scientist of Darwin's, made up the phrase "survival of the fittest." The phrase has since been used to suggest that human society is a battle for the "survival of the fittest." This theory is called Social Darwinism.

According to Social Darwinism, people compete with one another to survive, and the "fittest" people become richer and own more property. The theory suggests that poverty proves a person or group's weakness.

Many people do not agree with the theory of Social Darwinism. They believe that it does not consider many other

LEFT: *Herbert Spencer (1820–1903) in about 1890. Spencer agreed with Darwin's theory of evolution. He also believed that it could explain how human society evolved over time, from simple ways of life to complex industrial societies.*

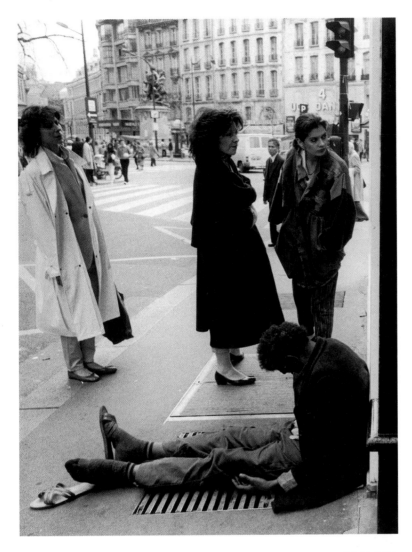

LEFT: *Shoppers in Paris ignore a homeless man who is sitting on a heat vent to keep warm. According to the theory of Social Darwinism, poverty is a result of natural selection, so it is part of nature. Many people disagree with this theory.*

influences on wealth and poverty, such as the family into which you are born, and events in history.

Despite the debate over Social Darwinism, few people would disagree that Darwin's groundbreaking theory of evolution was an important contribution to modern science. Darwin would have been happy to know that his discoveries made it possible for us to understand ourselves better than ever before.

IN THEIR OWN WORDS

"Our ancestor was an animal which breathed water, had a swim bladder, a great swimming tail, an imperfect skull, and undoubtedly was a hermaphrodite [both male and female]!"

DARWIN TO CHARLES LYELL ABOUT THE ANIMAL ORIGINS OF HUMANS, IN 1861.

Timeline

1798

Thomas Malthus writes an essay about how food supply cannot keep up with the growth of population. Darwin later uses these ideas when thinking about natural selection.

1801

Jean-Baptiste Lamarck publishes his early ideas on evolution. He says that animals change to adapt to their environment and pass on the changes to their offspring.

1809

FEBRUARY 12: Charles Darwin is born.

1815

JUNE 18: The Duke of Wellington defeats Napoleon at the Battle of Waterloo.

1817

JULY 15: Susannah Darwin, Charles' mother, dies.

1818

SEPTEMBER: Darwin is sent to boarding school.

1822

Rapid growth of cloth-producing factories in northwest England and lowland Scotland.

1824

Trade unions are allowed in England.

1825

The first steam railway service begins.

OCTOBER: Darwin goes to Edinburgh University.

1828

JANUARY: Darwin moves to Cambridge University.

1830

The first volume of Charles Lyell's *Principles of Geology* is published.

1831

DECEMBER: The H.M.S. *Beagle* sets sail on its voyage around the world.

1832

The Reform Act gives middle-class men over the age of 21 the right to vote in Great Britain.
DECEMBER: The *Beagle* lands at Tierra del Fuego, South America.

1835

FEBRUARY: Darwin sees an earthquake in Chile.
SEPTEMBER–DECEMBER: The *Beagle* visits the Galápagos Islands, Tahiti, and New Zealand.

1836

JANUARY: The *Beagle* lands in Australia.

OCTOBER 2: The *Beagle* arrives in Falmouth, England.

1837

Victoria is crowned Queen of the United Kingdom of Great Britain and Ireland.
Building of railway begins in Britain.
Darwin begins working on his theory of evolution.

1838

The Chartist movement demands the vote for workers.

1839

JANUARY 29: Charles Darwin and Emma Wedgwood are married.
Darwin's *Journal of Researches*, about the *Beagle* voyage, is published.
DECEMBER: The Darwins' first child, William, is born.

1842

SEPTEMBER: The Darwins move to Down House in Kent.

1844

Darwin writes an essay containing his theory of evolution, and sends it to Joseph Hooker.

1846

Darwin begins an eight-year study of barnacles.
The potato famine hits Ireland and also affects England and Wales. The farmers on Darwin's land are affected.
The British Government ends the Corn Laws to reduce the tax on bread.

1848

Revolutions sweep across Europe. Last big Chartist demonstrations occur in England. The Chartist movement collapses.

1851

APRIL: Charles' daughter, Annie, dies.
The Great Exhibition is held in London. Many of Britain's new industrial machines and goods are displayed to visitors.

1854

Britain and France join Turkey in the Crimean War against Russia.

1855

In Moravia, Gregor Mendel begins his studies of peas and how features are passed on from generation to generation.

1856

Henry Bessemer invents a way of making large amounts of steel very cheaply.
Darwin starts writing *The Origin of Species*.

1858

JUNE 18: Darwin receives a letter from Alfred Russel Wallace in which Wallace describes his theory of evolution.

JUNE 30: A joint paper on evolution by Wallace and Darwin is presented at the Linnean Society in London.

1859

Darwin's book about natural selection, *The Origin of Species*, is published.

1860

Debate in Oxford takes place between Bishop Sam Wilberforce and Darwin's supporters.

1861

The states of Italy form one country.
The American Civil War begins.

1862

Thomas Huxley publishes *Man's Place in Nature*, in which he argues that humans have ape origins.

1867

The Second Reform Act allows every house-owning man in Britain to vote.
The German philosopher Karl Marx publishes the first volume of *Das Kapital*.

1870

In England, the Education Act says that all 5 to 12 year-olds should attend school.

1871

The states of Germany form one country, the German Empire.
Darwin's book, *The Descent of Man*, is published.

1872

Darwin's book, *The Expressions of the Emotions in Man and Animals*, the third of his books on evolution, is published.

1876

Charles and Emma become grandparents, but Amy, the wife of their son Francis, dies shortly after giving birth.

1882

APRIL: Charles Darwin dies and is buried in Westminster Abbey.

1884

The Third Reform Act allows more than 2 million men in Britain to vote.

1900

The work of Gregor Mendel is recognized by scientists.

1996

Dolly the sheep becomes the world's first clone of a mammal.

Glossary

Adapted
Suited. Animals and plants are adapted, or suited to their environment.

Ancestor
An earlier type of animal or plant from which others have evolved.

Barnacles
Small sea animals with a hard shell, which stick to rocks and the bottom of ships.

Botanist
A scientist who studies plants.

Clergyman
A person, minister, pastor, rector, priest, or rabbi who does religious work.

Democratic
Allowing all the people a say in how a country is ruled.

Domestic
A domestic animal is a type of animal that has been tamed so it can be useful to people. Farm animals are domesticated animals.

Dominant
Most powerful.

Evolution
The process of change over time.

Extinct
Died out; no longer living in the world.

Fossils
Usually the hard parts of plants and animals, such as bones, shells, or bark, that have left impressions or remained in rock.

Genetics
The study of how features are passed on from parents to offspring.

Geologist
A scientist who studies the features of Earth's crust.

Iguanas
Large lizards.

Inbreeding
Breeding from closely related animals or people.

Indigenous
The first people to live in a place.

Memoirs
A person's writing about their memories of certain events or people.

Missionaries
People who travel to other countries to convert people to their religion.

Naturalist
A scientist who studies animals and plants.

Offspring
Children of animals or people.

Orchids
An orchid is a kind of flower. There are many different types of orchids in tropical countries.

Parish
An area that has its own church.

Postage franks
Marks on a letter to show that someone has paid for postage, like stamps.

Predators
Animals that feed on other animals.

Species
Animals or plants that have been grouped together because they share similar features. Members of a species can breed with each other but not with other species.

Specimens
Animals, plants, rocks, or other things that a scientist takes away so that he or she can learn about them.

Zoology
The study of animals.

Further Information

BOOKS FOR YOUNGER READERS

Fullick, Ann. *Groundbreakers: Charles Darwin*. Crystal Lake, IL: Heinemann, 2000.

Harris, Nicholas. *The Story of Life on Earth*. Brookfield, CT: Millbrook Press, 1999.

BOOKS FOR OLDER READERS

Milner, Richard. *Charles Darwin: Evolution of a Naturalist*. New York: Facts on File, 1994.

WEBSITES

Charles Darwin Time Line
http://honors.ccsu.ctstateu.edu/Honors/EText/Darwin/DarwinTimeLine.html
Time line of his life, with links to other sites.

www.darwinfoundation.org/misc/kids/kids.html
Information on Galápagos Islands for kids, including fun facts about the animals and plants that can only be found there.

Lycos
www.lycos.com
Use the search engine to find links to a biography site, a multimedia article, and other websites on Darwin.

VIDEOS

Charles Darwin—His Life, Journeys, and Discoveries (Cromwell Publications, 1999)

Discovery Channel—Galápagos—Beyond Darwin (Video Collection Int. Ltd, 1998)

Index

Page numbers in **bold** are pages where there is a photograph or an illustration.

JB
Darw

Senker, Cath
Charles Darwin

AWESOME ATHLETES

TOM BRADY

Jill C. Wheeler

ABDO Publishing Company

visit us at
www.abdopublishing.com

Published by ABDO Publishing Company, 4940 Viking Drive, Edina, Minnesota 55435.
Copyright © 2007 by Abdo Consulting Group, Inc. International copyrights reserved in all
countries. No part of this book may be reproduced in any form without written permission from
the publisher. The Checkerboard Library™ is a trademark and logo of ABDO Publishing
Company.

Printed in the United States.

Cover Photo: Corbis
Interior Photos: AP/Wide World pp. 4, 6, 7, 9, 12, 17, 21, 24, 25, 26, 27; Corbis pp. 13, 16,
   20, 23, 28-29; Getty Images pp. 5, 14, 16, 19, 22; Wire Image pp. 11, 15, 18

Series Coordinator: Rochelle Baltzer
Editors: Rochelle Baltzer, Megan Murphy
Art Direction: Neil Klinepier

Library of Congress Cataloging-in-Publication Data

Wheeler, Jill C., 1964-
  Tom Brady / Jill C. Wheeler.
     p. cm. -- (Awesome athletes)
  Includes index.
  ISBN-10 1-59928-305-0
  ISBN-13 978-1-59928-305-0
  1. Brady, Tom, 1977- 2. Football players--United States--Biography--Juvenile literature. 3.
Quarterbacks (Football)--United States--Biography--Juvenile literature. 4. New England Patriots
(Football team)--Juvenile literature. I. Title. II. Series.

GV939.B685W484 2007
796.332092--dc22

                                                                    2005035428

Contents

Tom Brady

Tom Brady is one of the brightest stars in the **National Football League (NFL)**. He has led the New England Patriots to three **Super Bowl** victories. He has twice been named the Super Bowl's Most Valuable Player (MVP). And, he is already being compared to football greats Joe Montana, John Elway, and Steve Young.

Brady's regular-season winning percentage is the best of any quarterback in Super Bowl history. Brady is known for staying calm under pressure. His passes are usually right on target. And, his coach says no one works harder than Tom Brady does.

Brady is a superstar off the field, too. He has hosted *Saturday Night Live* and been a guest on the *Late Show with David Letterman*. Brady has even appeared in cartoon form on

Brady's dedication, accuracy, and pure talent have helped to make him one of the NFL's most popular football players.

The Simpsons! Aside from his television appearances, Brady has spent time with President George W. Bush and Pope John Paul II.

Despite his celebrity status, Brady prefers to stay out of the spotlight. He keeps close relationships with his family and friends. Brady says he's still sometimes amazed at how his life has turned out.

Teammates praise Brady for his leadership skills. As a quarterback, Brady often leads his teammates during games.

Young Football Fan

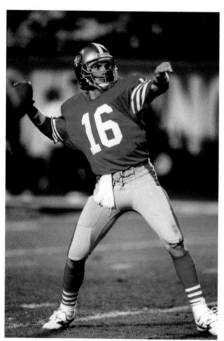

The Bradys were fans of the San Francisco 49ers. Quarterback Joe Montana was Tom's hero.

Thomas Edward Brady Jr. was born on August 3, 1977, in San Mateo, California. This city is near San Francisco. Tom's father, Tom Sr., was an investment banker. His mother, Galynn, was a homemaker. Tom has three older sisters named Maureen, Julie, and Nancy.

Growing up with three sisters was not always easy for Tom. He remembers when his sisters used to make him dress up and play dolls with them. Today, they still call him "Tommy."

The Brady family loves sports. Throughout the years, Tom's sisters played soccer and softball. Tom Sr. often helped coach their teams. Tom played football and baseball. One year, the four Brady children played in a total of 315 games!

Tom's interest in football started when he was young. When Tom was just four years old, his father took him to the National Football Conference (NFC) championship game.

Soon, Tom began playing football with his neighbors. He often pretended to be Joe Montana or Steve Young. Little did he know that one day he would be the football hero admired by children!

Tom remembers what it was like to look up to a sports figure. So today, he takes time to pose with fans.

High School Athletics

Tom attended Junipero Serra High School in San Mateo. It was an all-boys Catholic high school. Tom played on the school's football team. However, the Junipero Serra Padres were not very good. They had a record of 0–8 when Tom entered the school.

Tom loved football, but he did not succeed at it right away. However, he later improved enough to become a football champion at the school. Tom also enjoyed playing baseball. He earned **letters** in both baseball and football while at Junipero Serra. Aside from success on the fields, Tom was also a good student.

In 1995, Tom graduated from Junipero Serra High. Then, the Montreal Expos **drafted** him in the 1995 Major League Baseball draft. The Expos wanted Tom as a catcher. But Tom had other dreams. He wanted to play football.

Luckily, Tom had the chance to follow his dream. Earlier, his father had sent videotapes of Tom's football career to a number of colleges. Eventually, Tom accepted a **scholarship** from the University of Michigan in Ann Arbor.

Tom excelled in both baseball and football. But it was football that he felt most drawn to.

Playing for Michigan

Tom began classes at Michigan in fall 1995. Off the field, he **majored** in organizational studies. On the field, he was a backup quarterback for the Wolverines. He sat on the bench during his first year. This way, he was able to observe the players and learn more about the game.

Tom did not get much playing time in the 1996–1997 and 1997–1998 seasons either. He remained a backup for the starting quarterbacks. He played in just six games during those two seasons.

Yet even as a backup, Tom's talent was apparent. During those seasons, he threw a total of 20 passes. He completed 15 of those passes with no **interceptions**!

In January 1998, Tom helped lead the Wolverines to win the Rose Bowl. The Rose Bowl, the Citrus Bowl, and the Orange Bowl are annual postseason games played between U.S. colleges.

Opposite Page: Tom was becoming a valuable player for the Wolverines. Yet in his early college years, he felt frustrated about his limited playing time. He even thought about transferring schools. But his family and his coach encouraged him to stay.

In fall 1998, Tom won the starting position over previous quarterback Scott Dreisbach. He also beat out young sensation Drew Henson.

Tom's first season as starting quarterback for the Wolverines did not begin favorably. In a game against Syracuse University, the Wolverines lost in front of 111,000 fans. At one point, the Wolverines were down 38–7. Tom was benched and Drew was sent in. Fortunately, Drew made enough gains for a final score of 38–28.

Brady with fellow quarterbacks Drew Henson (left) and Jason Kapsner (middle) in August 1999

But as that season progressed, Tom proved that he belonged on the field. The Wolverines finished the 1998 season with ten wins and three losses. They went on to win the Citrus Bowl in January 1999.

Tom became cocaptain of the team for the 1999 season. He completed 62 percent of his passes that season, 20 of

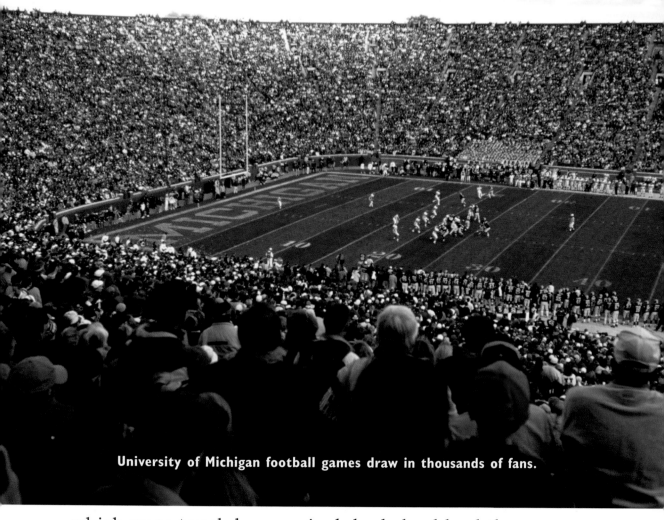

University of Michigan football games draw in thousands of fans.

which were touchdowns. And, he helped lead the Wolverines to an Orange Bowl victory in January 2000.

Tom graduated from the University of Michigan in spring 2000. By the end of his college career, Tom had posted 20 wins and only 5 losses as a starting quarterback.

To New England

During the 2000 NFL draft, one scout claimed Brady was too thin and that he lacked a strong arm. Brady proved the scout wrong during training camp.

In April 2000, Brady participated in the annual **NFL draft**. The New England Patriots chose him during the sixth round. He was the 199th player that the NFL accepted.

Brady played well during training camp with the Patriots. Yet he was still not sure he would make the team. Even if he did, he would be the team's fourth quarterback. And, Drew Bledsoe would continue as starter.

Fortunately, Brady made the team. But, he sat on the bench for all but one game during the 2000 season. The Patriots finished that season at the bottom of the American Football Conference (AFC) East, with 5 wins and 11 losses.

Brady was determined to improve. So during the off-season, he watched game films of the team's competitors. He practiced throwing to become more **accurate**. And, he spent many hours in the weight room. He bulked up from 204 pounds (93 kg) to 220 pounds (100 kg).

Brady bettered his game enough to become the team's backup quarterback for the 2001 season. He played in some preseason games. Both coaches and fans began to notice his incredible calmness under pressure.

Brady gets ready to pass during pregame drills in July 2000

Tom Brady is the youngest player to have twice been named the Super Bowl's Most Valuable Player.

1977	1995	1998	2000
Born on August 3 in San Mateo, California	Turns down a catcher's position with the Montreal Expos	Earns starting quarterback position for the University of Michigan Ann Arbor Wolverines	Graduates from the University of Michigan Ann Arbor

How Awesome Is He?

Brady is skilled at reading the opposing team and making quick decisions. He is also an excellent leader and a fierce competitor. Brady was rated number one in the 2005 regular season for passing yards.

Player/Ranking	Passing Yards
Tom Brady/#1	**4,110 (3,758 m)**
Trent Green/#2	4,014 (3,670 m)
Brett Favre/#3	3,881 (3,549 m)
Carson Palmer/#4	3,836 (3,508 m)

TOM BRADY

TEAM: NEW ENGLAND PATRIOTS
NUMBER: 12
POSITION: QUARTERBACK
HEIGHT: 6 FEET, 4 INCHES
WEIGHT: 225 POUNDS

2000	2001	2002	2004–2005
Drafted by the New England Patriots in sixth round	Becomes starting quarterback for the New England Patriots	Leads the Patriots to victory in Super Bowl	Wins second and third Super Bowls

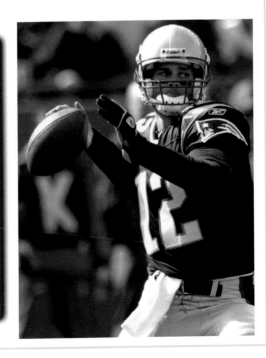

- Turned down a professional baseball career to attend the University of Michigan

- At age 24, became the youngest quarterback ever to lead a team to an NFL Super Bowl victory

- Signed a $60 million contract extension with the New England Patriots in 2005

Highlights

Starting Role

The second game of the 2001 season marked the start of many changes for Brady. The Patriots played against the New York Jets. During the game, Bledsoe suffered a serious chest injury. Brady was sent in to replace him. The Patriots didn't win, but Brady played successfully.

Patriots coach Bill Belichick had Brady start the next seven games while Bledsoe recovered. Brady performed so well that he remained starter even after Bledsoe had healed. The Patriots won 11 of their next 14 games! Brady was a strong leader, and he handled losses as gracefully as wins.

Under Brady's leadership, the Patriots won in overtime against the Oakland Raiders. This was the

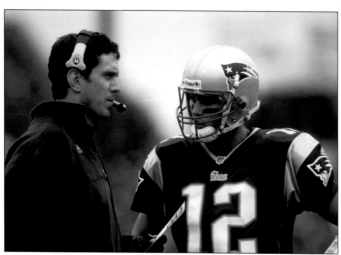

Bledsoe talks to Brady on the field

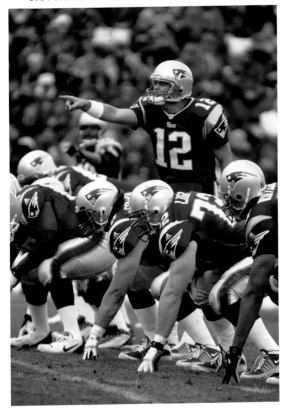

Brady signals during a game against the Cleveland Browns in December 2001

final game of the AFC divisional **play-offs**.

Next, the Patriots faced the Pittsburgh Steelers for the AFC title. Unfortunately, Brady sprained his ankle during the game and had to sit out. Bledsoe claimed the win. Still, the Patriots would play in the **Super Bowl**!

Despite Brady's injury, Belichick tagged him as starting quarterback for the 2002 Super Bowl against the St. Louis Rams. Some people questioned Belichick's choice. In the history of football, only two first-year starting quarterbacks had ever led their teams to a Super Bowl victory. Brady would need to beat the odds to defeat the Rams.

A Superstar Emerges

The 2002 **Super Bowl** was a close game. With just a minute and a half left to play, the Patriots and the Rams were tied at 17 points. The audience was tense.

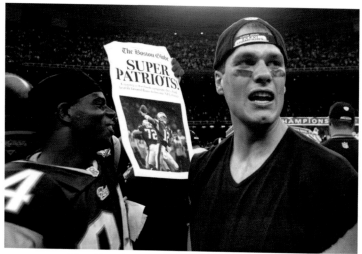

The Patriots celebrate their victory

Brady remained calm and began an offensive attack. He completed five of six passes to gain 53 yards (48 m). The Patriots were in **field goal** position in the final seconds of the game. Then, their kicker made a field goal to end the game at 20–17. The Patriots had won their first Super Bowl!

Brady had beat the odds. At 24, he was now the youngest quarterback to ever win a Super Bowl. He was also named the Super Bowl's MVP.

Suddenly, Brady had become a sports sensation! His name was everywhere. Next, he traveled to Hawaii to play in the Pro Bowl. This is the all-star game played at the end of a regular season. Only the best football

Brady was in a parade at Disney's MGM Studios the day after the 2002 Super Bowl. It is tradition for the Super Bowl MVP to visit a Disney theme park following the game.

players get to compete. Then in March, he was a judge in the 2002 Miss USA Pageant.

In April, Brady and the rest of the Patriots visited the White House. Then in May, Brady was named one of *People* magazine's 50 Most Beautiful People of 2002. And that summer, he even met his hero Joe Montana.

Now, almost everyone knew who Tom Brady was. People asked Brady for his **autograph** everywhere he went. This instant fame was quite a change for Brady. Sometimes it was overwhelming.

The Patriots visit the White House

Brady turned to his family for help. As always, they were supportive. They often visited him. And, Brady's sister Nancy moved to Boston, Massachusetts, to work as his personal assistant for a while. Two years later, the entire Brady family watched in delight as the Patriots won a second **Super Bowl**! Brady was also named MVP of the 2004 Super Bowl.

Brady holds his second Super Bowl trophy

Playing On

Brady's second **Super Bowl** victory earned him another visit to the White House. This time, he was a guest at President Bush's 2004 State of the Union address. And later that year, Brady met Pope John Paul II during a visit to Rome, Italy.

On the field, Brady's **dedication** and leadership continued to shine. Once again, he helped lead the Patriots to the 2005 AFC championship game. The team was scheduled to play against the Pittsburgh Steelers.

Tom Brady meets Pope John Paul II

Unfortunately, Brady became ill just days before the game. He had a temperature of 103 degrees Fahrenheit (39°C). The night before the game, he thought he might not even be able to play. Yet despite being sick, Brady made it on to the field. He helped the Patriots win 41–27. Now, the team had a chance to gain another **Super Bowl** victory!

A few weeks later, Brady's grandmother died. Brady was very close to her. Her death was a great loss for the entire Brady family. Despite his personal obstacles, Brady played well in the Super Bowl game against the Philadelphia Eagles. He led the Patriots to their third Super Bowl victory in four years!

The streets of Boston overflowed with Patriots fans when they celebrated the team's victory in the 2005 Super Bowl.

Brady Today

Brady continues to rely on his family when being a superstar athlete becomes too overwhelming. He jokes that trips to the post office or the grocery store no longer take a few minutes. Now, they last much longer as he talks to fans and signs **autographs**.

When Brady wants time out of the spotlight, he retreats to Gillette Stadium. This is where the Patriots practice and play home games. Brady also spends time alone watching game films to memorize the plays of opposing teams.

Brady is a modest superstar. He has turned down individual **sponsors** because he does not

Brady arrives at Patriots owner Robert Kraft's home in June 2005 with his guest, actress Bridget Moynahan. The Patriots were invited there to receive their Super Bowl rings.

want the attention. This decision has also helped him keep close relationships with his teammates. During summers, Brady and some of his teammates help coach local sports camps.

Other than playing football, Brady enjoys spending time with his family and playing golf. One of his wilder dreams is to run for a seat in the U.S. Senate.

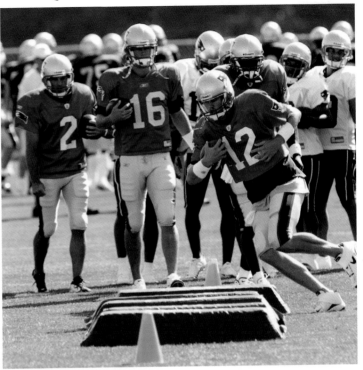

Football champions work hard to improve themselves on the field. Brady trained with his teammates at the Gillette Stadium in July 2005.

After his 2002 **Super Bowl** victory, Brady confessed that his biggest fear was to become a "one-hit wonder." But since then, this rising star has found there are endless possibilities.

Glossary

accurate - free of errors.

autograph - a person's handwritten name.

dedication - a commitment to a goal or a way of life.

draft - an event during which sports teams choose amateur players.

field goal - a kick made over the crossbar in football. It is worth three points.

intercept - to gain possession on an opponent's pass in football.

letter - the initial of a school awarded to a student for achievement, usually in athletics.

major - to focus on a particular subject or field of study in college.

National Football League (NFL) - a professional football organization in the United States consisting of the National Football Conference (NFC) and the American Football Conference (AFC). Each conference has 16 teams.

play-off - a series of games played after the end of a regular sports season to determine which teams will compete in a championship.

scholarship - a gift of money to help a student pay for instruction.

sponsor - someone who pays for a program or an activity in return for promotion of a particular product or brand.

Super Bowl - the NFL championship game played annually by the winners of the American and National football conferences.

Web Sites

To learn more about Tom Brady, visit ABDO Publishing Company on the World Wide Web at **www.abdopublishing.com**. Web sites about Brady are featured on our Book Links page. These links are routinely monitored and updated to provide the most current information available.

Index